JUST A THOUGHT
THE SMILEY REPORT
First Edition
1991-93

Tavis Smiley

PINES ONE PUBLISHING
LOS ANGELES, CALIFORNIA

Book Design: Wazir Aziz, Renaissance Graphics
Photos: Haywood Galbreath, H.G. Star-1 Photo
Library of Congress Cataloging-in-Publication Data
Smiley, Tavis, 1964-
just a thought, the smiley report, first edition/by Tavis
Smiley
p.cm.
All commentaries originally broadcast between 1991 and
1993 over Los Angeles radio and television.
ISBN: 0-9636952-3-1

Pines One Publishing
3870 Crenshaw Blvd., Suite 391
Los Angeles, CA 90008
(213) 290-1182

To: Emory G. Smiley, Joyce Smiley, Daisy M.
        Robinson, Pam, Phyllis, Garnie, Paul, Patrick,
        Maury, Dubby, Scooter and Dion

"Hast thou not known? hast thou not heard, that the everlasting God, the Lord, the Creator of the ends of the earth, fainteth not, neither is weary? there is no searching of his understanding.

He giveth power to the faint; and to them that have no might he increaseth strength.

Even the youths shall faint and be weary, and the young men shall utterly fall:

But they that wait upon the Lord shall renew their strength: they shall mount up with wings as eagles; they shall run, and not be weary; and they shall walk, and not faint."

Isaiah 40: 28-31

TABLE OF CONTENTS

TABLE OF CONTENTS

Charitable Contribution
Ordering Information

Acknowledgements

If I took the space necessary to adequately acknowledge all the persons whose involvement and support have made this book possible, there would be little room to print these selected essays.

I grew up in Indiana, one of ten children. Not unlike most people I've met who come from large families, it is only when you grow older that you truly appreciate a unique experience that others can best understand when they visit your family home during the holiday season. Memories of the past abound, hopes for the future are renewed and laughter fills the air.

Indeed those who know me best know that I'm happiest when talking about my family, particularly brothers Maury and Derwin who will graduate from Morehouse College and Hampton University respectively next spring.

My family, more than anything else, has been the primary source of my motivation to achieve. This book is dedicated to them.

In a very real way, this book is part of a journey that I fully expect will become more challenging and rewarding as I continue to travel. Along the way, a number of people continue to be unbelievably supportive as I pursue my goals.

First, I must acknowledge my publisher and partner, Denise Pines, who has been invaluable in the producing of this book.

Former Los Angeles mayor Tom Bradley was often criticized for not having groomed young progressive leadership to follow in his footsteps. While I do not purport to speak for Mr. Bradley, I can only say he has always supported my efforts and in fact gave me my entree into Los Angeles politics.

The Smiley Report did not create itself, nor does it remain on the air without the involvement of a host of individuals. I receive the constant support of friends and colleagues who challenge my thinking on most issues and help to focus and crystallize the message that eventually broadcasts over the airwaves.

My thanks to Craig Wilbraham and Liz Kiley of 92.3 THE BEAT for their belief in and support for The Smiley Report. Special thanks to Art Morrison and Glenn Marra at THE BEAT for making me sound reasonably articulate.

Before THE BEAT, The Smiley Report was originally broadcast over Los Angeles radio stations KGFJ 1230 AM and KJLH 102.3 FM. My thanks to both stations.

I've basically had a one-person staff since leaving the mayor's office in September of 1990. Lillie Murphy-Guthrie has been the most patient and understanding assistant anyone could ever have. Lillie has worked for me not because of the money, but because she believes in me. (I know it's time to change that Lillie. Let's hope people buy this book!)

I'm still somewhat new to the KABC-TV family, but I now know why Channel 7 is number one in Southern California...the personnel. Thank you Ernie Thornton, Roger Bell, Jim Hattendorf, Jim Huntington, Alice Morris and the entire Eyewitness News team.

Finally, the most important people...my abiding friends. Thank you Wazir Aziz, David W. Beall, Chi Blackburn, Tracey Brown, Wendi Chavis, Eula Collins, Paul Delpit, Willis Edwards, Rev. Kenneth J. Flowers, Brigette Fornis, "Big George" Hughley, Ralph and Ruth Isaacs, Daniel and Denise Lamaute, Michael Lyles, Marvelous Mack, Julianne Malveaux, Mike Mann, Bishop Robert W. McMurray, Harold and Beatrice Patrick, David and Betty Peterson, Aubrey Prince, Curtis Rossiter, Pat Russell, Kim Showell, Stephanie E. Williams and everyone else I love but didn't have the space to mention.

Tavis Smiley
Los Angeles
July, 1993

FOREWORD

I have only just a minute
Only sixty seconds in it
Forced upon me — can't refuse it
Didn't seek it, didn't choose it
But it's up to me to use it
I must suffer if I lose it
Give account if I abuse it
Just a tiny little minute
But eternity is in it

— Dr. Benjamin E. Mays

What can you do with a minute? Five days a week on THE BEAT, Tavis Smiley offers "just a thought," his commentary on the world as he knows it, on Los Angeles politics, world affairs, race, music, national politics. From time to time, he has offered tribute to special individuals, such as his friend and mentor, former Los Angeles mayor Tom Bradley. At other times, he has offered musings about gender relations, the Los Angeles police brutality verdicts, and other matters. Smiley's comments are those of a "reasoned" young black man, juggling pragmatism with anger and disbelief, taking the obvious and twisting it into "just a thought." His thoughts, sometimes trite, sometimes wise, represent a good use of his minute.

There is an adage that opinions are like noses — everybody has one. Everybody doesn't have the discipline to write them down, to shape them into a body of work, or the opportunity to have their opinion printed or broadcast. Tavis Smiley created his opportunity on THE BEAT, guessing that somewhere in a music format there would be just a minute to pause for his thought, for commentary on matters that transcend the slamming beat of hip-hop, pop, rhythm and blues.

Because I've been impressed by his ability to create opportunity, his tenacity and discipline, I was pleased that he asked me to write this foreword to his work.

This is a terrific time to be a pundit, a terrific time to raise one's voice. With the crumbling of the Berlin Wall, the reconfiguration of the race debate, simmering tension in cities, the budget deficit, international tensions in all these "former" countries, the former Soviet Union, the former Yugoslavia, President Clinton's recent bombing of Iraq, and the range of repercussions from the "end" of the Cold War, there is no shortage of things to talk about. Often absent at the table, though, are voices of color and younger voices. Tavis Smiley is among those who fill that void, both with his minute on THE BEAT, and with his regular commentary on KABC-TV (Channel 7). This collection documents that voice, and is the first of what will surely be a set of published commentaries by Tavis Smiley.

In saying this will be the first of a set of commentaries by Tavis Smiley, I pay tribute to a young man whose future possibilities are limitless. He has taken a fledgling political career and combined it with his record as a radio commentator to develop a voice that demands an audience, whether on radio or television. He bubbles over with energy, enthusiasm, and an optimism that is refreshing in a political arena that is turgid with cynicism. I value Tavis Smiley both as a "voice" and as a friend, especially as ours is a friendship that transcends gender, generation (I'm a boomer, he's a member of the floundering 13th generation), and political perspective (He's reasoned, I'm radical). Some of Tavis' commentary ticks me off, some of it tickles me, some of it takes my perspective on, but all of it provokes "just a thought," which is his goal.

My hat is off to Tavis Smiley for gathering his many well-used minutes into this collection of commentary. This is good work, a first step in what is likely to be a distinguished career, and a welcome new voice among pundits.

Julianne Malveaux
San Francisco
July, 1993

"The tragedy of life does not lie in not reaching your goal; the tragedy lies in having no goal to reach.

It isn't a calamity to die with dreams unfulfilled, but it is a calamity not to dream.

It is not a disaster to not be able to capture your ideals, but it is a disaster to have no ideals to capture.

It is not a disgrace to not be able to reach the stars, but it is a disgrace to have no stars to reach for.

Not failure — but low aim is sin."

Dr. Benjamin E. Mays

To Gerri from Gary,
It's always good
to RUN into a homegirl!
Thanks for your
support. Peace,

JUST A THOUGHT

Keep the Faith,

Tim Smiley

Never Again

April 21, 1993

Following the verdicts in the Rodney King civil rights trial, we continue our weeklong series, "Where Do We Go From Here?"

While the verdicts may represent a sense of hope for many of us, it must be said that the absence of another riot is not the presence of political and economic empowerment.

The verdicts will not make child care more affordable for single mothers...the verdicts will not create employment for young Black men in South Central...the verdicts will not provide health care for seniors...the verdicts will not improve education in the inner city.

I keep hearing people say it's time for us to put this incident behind us and move on.

WRONG.

Now is the time to turn up the heat on our elected officials, our community leaders and the powers that be.

We must stop allowing America to turn us on and off as if we were a television or a radio.

The Jews refuse to let us forget the Holocaust...the Japanese will not let us forget their internment during World War II...White America won't let us forget Elvis.

And we must not let this country ever forget the brutal beating of Rodney King.

Just a thought. I'm Tavis Smiley.

On Gun Control
(Part One)

February 27, 1992

For many African Americans who live in the inner city and almost daily come face to face with the violence caused by handguns and assault weapons, the issue of gun control is beginning to take center stage.

On one side of the issue are our traditional Black organizations like the NAACP and the Congressional Black Caucus, historically supporters of gun control legislation, citing the continual bloodshed and the carnage being wrought by automatic weapons in the hands of young gang members.

On the other side of the issue, we are beginning to see a growing number of Black elected officials like Mississippi Congressman Mike Espy becoming more supportive of the NRA's, (the National Rifle Association's) position of unrestricted gun ownership guaranteed by the Constitution.

Espy and others are urging the Black political establishment to move cautiously on the issue of gun control saying, essentially, that Blacks are the most likely to be victims of crime and the least likely to receive help from their local police department. They point to the Rodney King police beating as an example.

Additionally, the strong showing by David Duke in Louisiana's gubernatorial election last year has convinced even more Blacks that now is not the time to be advocating gun control.

More on this tomorrow.

Just a thought. I'm Tavis Smiley.

On Gun Control
(Part Two)

February 28, 1992

Should we ban the private ownership of all handguns as many are urging? Or will more restrictive laws such as imposing waiting periods for the purchase of handguns keep these deadly weapons out of the hands of would-be criminals in our community?

Yesterday, I pointed out that there is a growing number of respected Black leaders who are urging caution on this issue.

Recently in Virginia, the NAACP, American Civil Liberties Union and the National Rifle Association joined together to modify a law that would have prohibited people living in housing projects, predominately Blacks and Hispanics, from owning handguns.

This proposed legislation smacks of racism and a severe breach of equal protection under the law.

We would all like to live and raise our families in a society where the ever-present threat of death from a handgun wasn't lurking in air.

However, until we can develop a strategy to get rid of ALL privately-owned handguns, there should be a federally mandated waiting period to purchase these weapons.

Additionally, legislation should be enacted to require that individuals wanting to purchase a handgun be licensed and complete a course in responsible gun use and ownership.

Just a thought. I'm Tavis Smiley.

Twice Defeated

The U.S. Census Bureau recently released some good — but not so good — census figures.

The median figure for Black family incomes rose 84% from 1980 to $19,758 in 1990. Comparatively, white median household incomes climbed 60% to $31,435.

Additionally, the 1990 census found that among Blacks aged 25 and over, 63.1% had finished high school and 11.4% had completed college. Among Whites, 77.9% had finished high school and 21.5% had completed college.

Perhaps I've offered too many statistics too close together. It's really quite simple. Allow me to interpret.

If you're educated and White you make MO MONEY. If you're educated and Black you make NO MONEY.

The economic earnings of American Blacks still lag far behind those of equally educated Whites.

Without an education - you're twice defeated.

Despite these gruesome statistics, Malcolm X was right.

"Education is our passport to the future, for tomorrow belongs to the people who prepare for it today."

Just a thought. I'm Tavis Smiley.

Out of the Closet

January 27, 1993

It's been widely reported that President Bill Clinton will move to lift the ban on homosexuals in the military sometime tomorrow.

Clinton has said he will keep his campaign commitment despite growing opposition in Congress and without the support of the Joint Chiefs of Staff.

This issue has become a real "stinker" for the young President and potentially represents another embarrassing set back following the Zoe Baird incident.

As far us I'm concerned, the question isn't should there be gays in the military - obviously there already are. The question is will they be forced to continue lying about being gay?

A quick review of history reminds one that many of the same arguments used to keep Blacks out of the military have now resurfaced in the debate over gays in the military.

At one point America didn't want - indeed would not let - Blacks into the armed forces. Yet, when Muhammad Ali refused to fight in a war he opposed because of his religious beliefs, he was ostracized.

I can't figure it out.

If gays can be drafted to defend this country in wartime, they should be allowed to voluntarily enlist in the military during peacetime.

A strong sexual conduct policy should continue to be strictly enforced.

But otherwise, I've got a sneaky suspicion that come the next draft there'll be a whole lot of people coming out of the closet.

Just a thought. I'm Tavis Smiley.

Music to Whose Ears?

June 18, 1993

The designation of June as Black Music Month was a wonderful idea because it encourages radio stations all across America to remind each of us of the talents and undeniable contributions of African Americans to the music field.

But Black Music Month should be more than playing our favorite tunes from great artists like Marvin Gaye, Aretha Franklin and James Brown.

It seems to me that in addition to celebrating our past, Black Music Month should also foster a dialogue about the future of Black music.

Not long ago I aired a commentary in which I took exception to comments by a representative of a local theme park who blamed "rap music" for a violent outbreak at the park. The spokeswoman argued that rap music had attracted the wrong crowd of people, when in fact the scheduled rap concert had been miserably over-sold.

Rap music is a viable and wonderful art form that must be support-ed and — when necessary and appropriate — defended.

But we must also be willing to take a closer look at rap music that glorifies if not condones violence against law enforcement...has made the forty-ounce King...and refers to Black women as b_ _ _ _ _ _ and whores.

Just a thought. I'm Tavis Smiley.

Don't Balance the Budget on My Back

September 9, 1992

The Stanford Center for the Study of Families Children and Youth released a report yesterday which addressed the potential impact Proposition 165 could have on the children of California who receive support from the Aid to Families with Dependent Children program.

If passed in November, according to Governor Wilson, Prop 165 would reduce cash benefits for a mother and two children from $663.99 a month to $507 a month.

Wilson suggests that a mother working 6-10 hours a week at $5.00 an hour could make up the difference.

Now I'm no mathematician, but if a mother did work 10 hours a week at $5.00 an hour she'd gross about $200 a month.

Subtract money for transportation, clothing, a baby-sitter and, of course, - taxes - and the number on my calculator has a short horizontal line in front of it.

There's nothing wrong with encouraging mothers whose children derive support from AFDC to help themselves by finding a decent job.

But where? It's obviously been a while since Governor Wilson went job-hunting.

The Stanford study estimates that if Prop. 165 passes, more than half of the state's AFDC parents will be unable to find work.

More on this later.

Just a thought. I'm Tavis Smiley.

Environment = Economy

May 27, 1992

Next week, President Bush will join other world leaders in Rio de Janeiro for a global environmental summit. The summit has refocused attention on environmental issues.

In Los Angeles, protecting the environment has become a worthy crusade. A good number of Hollywood personalities have become spokespersons for environmental causes. Jane Fonda, Ed Begley Jr., Ted Danson and Kirstie Alley to name a few. Cheers to all of them!

However, I've long had three major criticisms of our local environmental movement.

One, in Los Angeles, the environmental movement is really a white, Westside, liberal movement. Organizers have not done enough to expand the core of the environmental leadership into other communities.

Two, although by now we've all heard the words "reduce, re-use and recycle," in the poor and minority communities this message isn't clearly understood. Not enough education on protecting our environment has been targeted at the indigenous community.

And, three, while environmental activists are long on understanding the problems of our environment, they are short on understanding the underlying economic reasons which lead to abuse of the environment.

Leaders of the environmental movement must begin to do a better job of linking the problems of our environment to the problems of our economy.

Just a thought. I'm Tavis Smiley.

Take Bigotry off the Menu

May 25, 1993

Yesterday, Denny's announced that the manager of an Annapolis, Maryland, restaurant had been fired for failing to report an incident of race bias.

Last month, six Black Secret Service agents waited almost an hour for their breakfasts. White Secret Service officials who arrived with them were served within ten minutes by the same waitress. The six Black agents eventually left hungry.

At the time of this Annapolis incident, the Denny's chain was already facing a lawsuit here in California based on similar complaints from over thirty African American customers.

What's up with Lenny's...I mean Denny's?

The restaurant chain has denied that these incidents constitute a pattern of racism.

How many more incidents of discrimination will it take for Denny's to wake up and smell the coffee?

There's one sure way to convince Denny's to take bigotry and discrimination off its menu.

Start eating at Lenny's instead of Denny's.

Just a thought. I'm Tavis Smiley.

Not Equal Giving — Equal Sacrifice

October 19, 1992

A few months ago, I offered five strategies for greater empowerment of America's economically and politically disenfranchised.

One of those five strategies was charitable giving. I argued that we need to do a better job of supporting the organizations and institutions that serve the least among us.

Last week Independent Sector, a coalition of corporations, foundations and volunteer groups, released a survey on charitable giving.

The survey found that the number of African Americans who made charitable contributions was up from 61% in 1989 to 64% in 1991. African Americans also gave the highest percentage of household income.

Volunteering by African Americans jumped to 43%, up from 38% in 1989.

Interestingly, the survey found that poorer people give more money proportionately than wealthier people. Contributors earning under $19,000 gave 4% of their income. Households earning $100,000 or more gave only 3%. This during a recession!

The next time one of my wealthier friends starts complaining again about how we're always trying to soak the rich, he'd better hope I'm not in the room.

Just a thought. I'm Tavis Smiley.

Hostages of Healthcare

February 11, 1993

Recently, the New England Journal of Medicine published a report which offers hope for a sickle cell anemia cure.

Sickle cell is a painful and deadly disease that afflicts more than 100,000 Americans, primarily those of African descent.

Researchers have found that injections of a common food additive can re-awaken a dormant gene and relieve the underlying cause of sickle cell anemia.

Dr. Douglas Faller of Boston University Medical School said, "The results are very exciting and dramatic. In every case, the patients treated...achieved levels of fetal hemoglobin that would be predicted to completely alleviate their disease."

The treatment is still considered experimental, and experts caution that much more study is needed.

Now that's good news.

Research, however, has been slowed because doctors have been unable to interest pharmaceutical companies in taking over production of the medicine because it would not be profitable.

Said one researcher, "It's purely economics. It's not racism."

Well, it may not be racist but it certainly is unconscionable.

Unconscionable that thousands of Americans are condemned to suffer and die because it's not profitable to produce the medicine that could cure them. There can be no clearer indictment of our nation's health care system.

We spend 30% more of our income on health care than any other nation. And yet, an estimated 100,000 people lose their health insurance every month. This doesn't include the 35 million Americans who have no basic health coverage.

President Clinton's effort to reform our nation's health care system is timely and long overdue.

To be sure, opposition from special interests and the powerful for-profit hospital lobby will make reform difficult.

It seems that some in the health care industry would rather treat disease than promote good health.

As the President's task force moves forward, Americans everywhere must demand that medical spending be slowed, that the uninsured be covered and that long-term care be extended to those in need.

We must declare that we are sick of the high cost of being sick.

Just a thought. I'm Tavis Smiley.

Lawyer-Bashing

July 8, 1993

Earlier this week, the president of the California State Bar Association called for a "cease fire" on lawyer-bashing.

In the aftermath of last week's shooting in a San Francisco law office, the Bar president argued that jokes against attorneys contribute to increased physical violence. There is, of course, no proof of his claim but why do people bash lawyers?

Maybe it's because there are too many of them in this country. The United States has more lawyers per 1,000 people than any other nation in the world.

It used to be that when you needed an attorney, you'd go find one. You don't have to look very far these days...they come to you. Through radio...through television and even in print advertisements. No stone is left unturned as lawyers market themselves as if they were athletic shoes or toothpaste.

Indeed, the Bar Association president admitted that lawyers may have been their own worst enemies by adopting their current marketing practices which emphasize the potential financial rewards a client can enjoy. And why? Because marketing oneself allows one to have a competitive edge...and thus make more money.

Two. No case is too frivolous to litigate. Your husband was a chainsmoker and died of lung cancer? No problem. Let's sue the tobacco companies. You thought your wife loved you but she really did not? No problem. Let's sue her.

Three. No amount of money is too great to seek for punitive damages. Two million? Ten million? Thirty million? Why do people bash lawyers?

For the record, I have nothing personal against lawyers. Some of my best friends are attorneys! But talk about making yourself an easy target!

The Bar president compared jokes against attorneys to hate speech against women and African Americans. As a solution to lawyer-bashing, he has suggested that crimes against attorneys should rate special penalties similar to crimes against police, judges and political officeholders.

First of all, I know of no one — prior to birth — who asked to be a woman. And African Americans know all too well that being Black is not a choice. People do, however, choose their professions.

And while I'm on the subject, why is it that everytime someone or some group seeks political or judicial redress African Americans are used as the litmus test? The basis upon which they define their struggle?

What happened in San Francisco last week is deeply disturbing and quite unfortunate...but crimes against attorneys should not rate special penalties while Blacks, women and others suffer most.

Now, I suppose I should go find an attorney to defend me against what the president of the California Bar will surely define as my hate speech against lawyers.

Just a thought. I'm Tavis Smiley.

How Long?

May 11, 1993

Yesterday, the Clinton Administration announced that it was putting the Bosnia situation on hold for a week because the Administration had failed to win the support of our European allies for stronger action to end the war.

President Clinton wants to supply arms to Bosnia's embattled Muslims and to bomb selected Bosnian Serb targets.

I don't know about you, but this Bosnian situation is a bit confusing.

I mean, you've got the Bosnian Serbs, the Muslims, the Croats, the Yugoslavian Serbs and the Macedonians in the Albanians.

Who's fighting who? Why are they fighting? And what are American servicemen and women about to get into?

The only thing I really know about the war in Bosnia-Herzegovina is that it once again highlights man's inhumanity to man.

In the final analysis, I guess that's all we really need to know.

President Clinton is right to demand that our allies join us in condemning and putting an end to the ethnic cleansing before we act unilaterally.

But how long must we wait for Europe's approval to do what we know is right?

Just a thought. I'm Tavis Smiley.

The Right Train of Thought

June 15, 1993

A few weeks ago, one of America's pioneering and most profitable Black-owned businesses was seized by a bankruptcy court.

The firm's founder, who died unexpectedly a few years ago, had committed that most basic sin which far too many people in our community are guilty of — not grooming a successor.

I've never understood it.

You'd think that as hard as we have to work to achieve a little something...we would be most serious about protecting and preserving what we've labored to build.

Over the weekend, I happened to catch "Soul Train" on Saturday.

I've often marveled at how Don Cornelius has kept Soul Train on the air consistently for so many years.

Last Saturday, Cornelius introduced a new co-host, Ken Taylor. Formerly of the E! Entertainment Channel and an on-air personality here at THE BEAT, Taylor will join Cornelius periodically to learn the ropes and one day wish us all Love...Peace...and Soul!

It's a smart move for Don Cornelius, a good move for Soul Train and a wonderful opportunity for a young brother.

Just a thought. I'm Tavis Smiley.

It's Wrong

October 20, 1992

Last week, a number of Asian Pacific groups joined the call for a reduction in the number of liquor stores in South Central Los Angeles.

Many of the inner city merchants whose businesses were destroyed during the civil unrest — mostly Korean Americans — have asked for financial assistance in exchange for converting the liquor outlets or relocating outside of South Los Angeles.

Some time ago, I aired a commentary blaming the City of Los Angeles for the ungodly number of liquor outlets in South Central Los Angeles.

At fault is the Los Angeles City Council.

Long ago, the council could have and should have taken steps to limit the number of liquor stores in this part of the city. The city has placed so many restrictions on adult entertainment establishments that you don't see them popping up everywhere.

Now that these Asian-American merchants are asking for money to relocate, the city has indicated that funds may not be available.

It's wrong to arbitrarily force certain merchants out of business by not allowing them to rebuild...it's wrong to have so many liquor stores in South Los Angeles...and it's wrong to not offer incentives to close down these suicide shops.

Just a thought. I'm Tavis Smiley.

The Lesser of Two Evils

October 29, 1992

Throughout Governor Bill Clinton's race for the White House, a small but vocal group of African American opinion makers have openly criticized Clinton for his attempt to shift the Democratic party away from its traditional liberal stance.

Clinton's campaign strategy has been to court the White voters, angry that the party has become too liberal, while promising to safeguard the gains by Blacks.

But as Clinton's lead has diminished, some of his Black critics have urged Black leaders to demand that Clinton publicly state his position on issues important to Blacks.

Clinton knows he can't do this and win. Yet, to not do it raises questions about his true commitment to African American issues.

Meanwhile, around the country most Black leaders have nonetheless declared their support for Governor Clinton. Some like Jesse Jackson have done so unenthusiastically, however, on the premise that Clinton is the lesser of two evils.

For me, the stakes are too high to vote for a presidential candidate just because he's the lesser of two evils.

Politically, at least, I understand Clinton's campaign strategy.

Practically, should Clinton win, I hope some real commitments have been made that we just don't know about.

The late James Baldwin put it this way, "Color is not a human or a personal reality, it is a political reality."

Just a thought. I'm Tavis Smiley.

R-E-S-P-E-C-T

March 10, 1993

This morning I was in one of the most important meetings of my life, along with three other gentlemen with whom I'm involved in a business venture.

I had literally begged for a meeting with the Senior V.P. of this company, who just happened to be a woman.

For that matter, one of the persons who I lobbied to get this meeting scheduled for me was another well-placed female.

As I drove away from the meeting, it occurred to me that my partners and I were at the mercy of a Black female corporate executive for the success or failure of this particular business endeavor.

Despite what we may say, I think Anita Hill scared many of us into fearing the Black woman as opposed to respecting the Black woman.

One of my friends joked after the Thomas/Hill fight that he was going to have women sign a form before leaving his office that they had not been harassed while inside.

There's a big difference between fearing and respecting.

If we did more of the latter, perhaps there would be less cause for the former.

Just a thought. I'm Tavis Smiley.

Short Arms & Heavy Ears

January 11, 1993

How often have you said to someone who's sharing something very personal or painful with you that, "I understand what you're going through."

If you're anything like me, probably more times than you can count.

But, if the truth be known, most often we don't "understand" what the person is going through, although we do "empathize" with their situation.

Over the past few years, I've spoken any number of times to groups of incarcerated young Black males.

Up until last week, I thought I "understood" what they and their families were going through.

Last Wednesday, one of my seven younger brothers was sentenced to serve a substantial amount of time in prison.

I can only say this. Understanding the presumed Black male crisis will require thinking more with our hearts and less with our heads.

Many of us are simply too quick to judge others using another man's values as our litmus test.

Whether we like it or not, these troubled young men and women belong to us.

Our arms must never be too short to save them, our ears never too heavy to hear them.

Just a thought. I'm Tavis Smiley.

Six Million Dollar Man

June 9, 1993

Well...at least it's over. No more of those "who do you trust" questions for a while.

Although Richard Riordan received the greatest number of votes yesterday, the "who do you trust" question still hasn't been answered definitively.

A Los Angeles Times exit poll found that 60% of Mike Woo's supporters voted for him because they had greater disdain for Dick Riordan...and about half of Mr. Riordan's supporters considered him the lesser of two evils.

Imagine that.

When the Beatles sang "Money Can't Buy You Love", they hadn't met Mayor-elect Richard Riordan.

Given the lack of real enthusiasm for either of yesterday's mayoral candidates, money most certainly made the difference.

Riordan had more money, and with it he bought more love.

Six months ago, voters didn't know who Dick Riordan was. They do today.

Dick Riordan: The man who became mayor by purchasing 56% of Los Angeles' affection for six million dollars.

Just a thought. I'm Tavis Smiley.

Wanted: The Truth

(Part One)

May 13, 1992

Earlier this week, two-hundred and fifty Oregonians asked the Senate Rules Committee to unseat Oregon Republican Bob Packwood, asserting that the senator lied about sexual accusations to win re-election.

Following the hearings, most senators seemed uncomfortable being asked by petitioners to penalize Mr. Packwood for allegedly lying to the press to delay publication of newspaper reports about the sexual harassment charges.

It seems to me that these petitioners have backed senators into a corner and have consequently ensured the defeat of their request.

Essentially, the Senate Rules Committee is being asked to decide whether lying to voters should negate an election victory?

Now...would any senator answer this question in the affirmative? Would Bill Clinton be President? Would George Bush have been President? Would Ross Perot have a chance of ever becoming President?

The issue here is whether or not Senator Packwood sexually harassed more than twenty women. Let's not waste time asking questions that we already know the answers to.

More on this tomorrow.

Just a thought. I'm Tavis Smiley.

Wanted: The Truth
(Part Two)

May 14, 1993

Oregon Republican Senator Bob Packwood is presently being investigated by both the Senate Rules Committee and the Ethics Committee for sexual misconduct.

At best, this smacks of double jeopardy...not to mention a waste of taxpayers' dollars.

Mr. Packwood should be thoroughly investigated, and that inquiry ought to be done by the Ethics Committee as I see it.

And speaking of the Ethics Committee...why is the Committee conducting virtually all of its work in secret?

When law professor Anita Hill made similar allegations against Clarence Thomas, their confrontation was promoted by the media — and the United States Senate — as if it were a prize fight.

Thomas vs. Hill.

In the final analysis, the people in Washington can ask all the questions but the people in Oregon have all the answers.

Recall him...vote him out...or re-elect him.

Ultimately, Oregon voters will have the last word...and that's the way it ought to be.

Just a thought. I'm Tavis Smiley.

Why Build Coalitions?

June 4, 1992

Tuesday's passage of Charter Amendment F, the police reform measure, was cause for celebration within the African American community.

The re-election of Judge Joyce A. Karlin was not.

After Karlin sentenced a Korean grocer to five years probation and a $500 fine for the killing of Latasha Harlins, Black leadership vowed to defeat her at the polls. In so doing, these leaders created an "us vs. them" political showdown.

Although narrow, the victory by Karlin reinforces a message that I've delivered before.

When any minority group in this city makes a unilateral decision to go to war with the city's White voting majority - they always lose. Because Los Angeles has such an ethnically diverse populous, no ethnic group can fight the power structure alone and win.

Proposition G, the controversial "Buy American" initiative, was to the city's Asian-Pacific population what the Karlin election was to the Black community. We both lost.

The message? Simple. Proposition F passed overwhelmingly because it was supported by a coalition which involved all of the city's ethnic groups.

Without a coalition, the chances of winning anything in Los Angeles are slim to none. And slim is out of town.

Just a thought. I'm Tavis Smiley.

There Goes the Neighborhood

May 28, 1993

Over the past few weeks, the Los Angeles City Council has wasted a lot of time debating an ordinance that would ban gang members from parks, playgrounds and beaches.

The council has temporarily tabled a measure that would make it a misdemeanor for gang members with two or more crimes on their records to enter any park, beach or playground with the intent of engaging in gang activity.

Clearly, gang activity cannot be condoned. Not at parks, playgrounds or beaches. But Angelenos must not be forced to tolerate gang activity in their neighborhoods either.

Most of the drive-by shootings that have taken place in this city have not occurred at tourist attractions, but rather in the streets of Los Angeles...in front of somebody's house...with kids perhaps playing in the yard.

When we make parks, playgrounds and beaches off-limits to gang members, we only contain the violence in certain areas of the city. Consequently, we force these gang members to "engage in gang activity" in somebody's backyard. Not yours or mine of course.

The problem with this proposal — like most proposals that target gang members — is that the measure is reactive rather than proactive.

It seems to me that if we want to keep young men out of gangs and prison on the backside of life, we must provide something positive and productive for them to do on the frontside of life.

An education and a job would be a good place to start.

Just a thought. I'm Tavis Smiley.

There, but for the grace of God...

July 24, 1992

A couple of days ago while pulling into my driveway, I noticed someone tearing open the garbage bags which I had sat outside earlier for the day's trash pick-up.

Quite naturally, I exited my vehicle and began to approach the individual to have a few words with them — or more accurately, at them — when I found myself looking into the face of an older woman who looked frighteningly like my 82 year-old grandmother who lives in Indiana.

The experience was so unreal that it somewhat scared me.

I was absolutely stunned. Here it was a beautiful day...I was feeling good about the distance I'd just run...and now I come home to see the face of my grandmother going through my garbage.

Needless to say, the lady was homeless.

As most of us move casually through another sunny Southern California summer...it's hard to imagine as I did the other morning, that the lady going through my trash might not be around next summer. Such is the nature of being homeless during wintry weather.

I don't rightly know what the point of this commentary is, other than to say that you'd be amazed at how much the homeless on our streets are looking more and more like you and I everyday.

Just a thought. I'm Tavis Smiley.

Knock. Knock.

June 22, 1993

Yesterday, in an 8 to 1 vote, the Supreme Court upheld the White House policy of denying Haitian refugees entrance into the United States.

During his campaign for the White House, Bill Clinton called the interception "cruel and unjust."

As President, Bill Clinton has maintained the Bush policy of returning the Haitians to their troubled homeland where many then face detention, abuse and death.

This particular White House policy is as racist as any we've seen in recent years.

We allow literally thousands of "political" refugees from other countries to apply for asylum, yet we force the Haitians to return home without even asking their reasons for fleeing.

Somehow, the 1991 overthrow of the first democratically elected President of Haiti in a military coup doesn't qualify "these people" to enter our borders as political refugees.

By the way...the one justice who voted in opposition was not Clarence Thomas.

Just a thought. I'm Tavis Smiley.

What If They Don't Riot?
(Part One)

April 5, 1993

Here lately we've been inundated with news stories and other incidents of riot preparedness by people all over the city.

Last Saturday, the <u>Los Angeles Times</u> reported that many Korean American business owners are stocking up on weapons and ammunition.

In Culver City, the police chief has urged residents to arm themselves for what he termed another riot worse that the first.

Los Angeles City Councilman and mayoral hopeful, Joel Wachs, has asked that the National Guard be on Los Angeles Streets before the verdicts are announced.

Last week, I told you that the Crusader Insurance Company dropped coverage for some 1,200 of its customers who own businesses in South Los Angeles.

Two weeks ago, I was in a meeting where two LAPD officers and one commander were present. When asked about the pending riot, one of the captains spoke up quickly urging us to take our loved ones and get out of town for a few days. The higher ranking commander said nothing.

The news media is on full alert ready to bring us extended live coverage just in case they riot.

Now, I'm still trying to figure out who they are, but what if they don't riot?

More on this tomorrow.

Just a thought. I'm Tavis Smiley.

What If They Don't Riot?

(Part Two)

April 6, 1993

Yesterday, I talked about all of the pre-riot preparations underway in Los Angeles County just in case they riot.

Now I still haven't figured out who they are, but what if they don't riot?

What if all the media hype doesn't compel people to burn down the city again?

What if certain business owners in South Los Angeles who've armed themselves take the law into their own hands and begin shooting people accidentally-on-purpose?

What if all the trash talked outside the federal court building by the defendants and their attorneys has fallen on deaf ears?

What if people want jobs and other economic opportunities in the inner city and not the National Guard?

What if people are pleased with the progress Chief Willie L. Williams is making and no longer have a desire to get back at former police chief Daryl Gates?

What if peace abounds and they don't riot?

Will this city return to business as usual, ignoring her economically and politically disenfranchised peoples?

Just a thought. I'm Tavis Smiley.

What If They Don't Riot?
(Part Three)

April 7, 1993

Over the last two days, you've heard me ask the question, "What if they don't riot?"

They, of course, are us. We who own nothing...we who have no voice...we who cannot control our emotions.

Well, for starters, you and I know better. We controlled our emotions for 27 years between the Watts Riots and last year's civil unrest.

All the while very little was changing. But that's the subject of another commentary...or two...or three.

For now, I'd like nothing more than to show this city and indeed the world that we will fight for the security of justice but with a different weapon.

Not with guns, not with molotov cocktails, not even with our hands. Rather, we will fight with our heads.

We will not give some trigger happy store owner a target...we will not give the news media another story to use as advertising bait...we will not give the politicians another excuse to deny us anything and everything we need or want.

Yes, we must fight. But we must choose the right weapon.

Just a thought. I'm Tavis Smiley.

Hoping against Hope

June 29, 1993

Last Friday, the Supreme Court overturned a ruling in favor of a fired Black prison supervisor and declared that an alleged victim of discrimination bears the "ultimate burden" of proving he was dismissed because of his race.

In the past, employers have had to convince the court that they had legitimate reasons for firing an employee.

Not anymore...thanks to Justice Clarence Thomas. Thomas voted with the majority in this 5 to 4 ruling which will make it practically impossible to win large class-action cases of discrimination.

I hate to take away a person's hope, because sometimes hope is all one has.

But those who had hoped that once confirmed Clarence Thomas would become more moderate and sensitive — should stop hoping.

It's as if Clarence Thomas wants Black America to pay for what he termed, "a high tech lynching" of a Black man during his confirmation hearings.

With each ruling, Clarence Thomas is lynching Black America.

And to think...the NAACP refused to even take a position on his nomination.

Just a thought. I'm Tavis Smiley.

Late Freight

December 28, 1992

This week on The Smiley Report, we pause to review a few of the most significant events of 1992.

Today, the U.N. sponsored action in Somalia.

A few weeks ago, I aired a commentary about Somalia that got me in a little trouble with a particular listener who somehow assumed that I was opposed to the U.S. presence in Somalia.

No, I'm not opposed to the U.S. efforts in Somalia. Only to our chest-beating about something we should have done a long time ago.

To practically ignore the starvation in Somalia and other countries for so many years is beyond my understanding. To now pat ourselves on the back about our humanitarian deeds is even worse.

Only the tortoise could have moved any slower.

But, I guess late is better then never.

And if there is something to be proud of, it is that the U.S. has undertaken a mission without a clearly identifiable vested interest.

No oil, no diamonds, no slave labor.

Humanitarian aid ought not be "quid pro quo" in the first place.

Here's to a timely return home for our troops and the successful completion of their mission.

More tomorrow.

Just a thought. I'm Tavis Smiley.

Did the Right Thing

May 7, 1993

Since the verdicts were rendered in the Rodney King civil rights trial, a number of people have been cashing in on their involvement in the high profile case.

Stacey Koon was paid to appear on "Hard Copy" and "Donahue". Lawrence Powell appeared on ABC's "Day 1", and no less than two of the jurors were also paid to appear on "Donahue".

I suppose to some this might be characterized as the American way, but it leaves a bad taste in my mouth.

Koon and Powell have argued that they've accepted these large sums of money because they have not received a salary for the better part of two years.

This argument, of course, ignores the fact that had they not deprived Rodney King of his civil rights they would no doubt still be gainfully employed by LAPD.

In any event, I guess that's why I was so pleased to learn that Juror #12, Martin De La Rosa, a grocery store clerk in Riverside, is using his celebrity to raise money for a scholarship fund in memory of a family friend.

Here's to Martin De La Rosa for doing the right thing. Twice.

Just a thought. I'm Tavis Smiley.

Commitment

August 25, 1992

Yesterday, I told a somewhat humorous story to make a point about commitment.

During last week's Republican National Convention, Mary Fisher, a woman infected with the AIDS virus, chided her party for its virtual silence on the deadly disease and challenged Republicans to commit themselves to spreading the word that AIDS can strike anyone.

Fisher ought to know. A mother of two boys, she contracted the disease from her ex-husband.

Said Fisher, "...the AIDS disease does not care whether you are Democrat or Republican, Black or White, male or female, gay or straight, young or old."

Today, some AIDS patients are being forced to sell their life insurance polices for a percentage of the value just to have money for care.

For example, selling a $100,000 policy might net an AIDS patient $60,000 in cash. Upon his or her death, the company collects the full amount of the policy — or put frankly — a $40,000 profit.

This practice is sick and exists primarily because of a lack of commitment on the part of our government to stop the spread of AIDS.

Time out for lip service. It's time to commit.

Just a thought. I'm Tavis Smiley.

The Joke's on You

May 21, 1993

Earlier this week, Republican State Assemblyman Pete Knight distributed a racist poem at a private meeting of Assembly Republicans.

When questioned by reporters about the poem, which mocks illegal immigrants for "breeding" as a hobby and driving out "the White man race", Mr. Knight called it interesting, clever and funny.

Well, the legislative Latino caucus didn't think it was so funny and asked Mr. Knight to make a public apology on the Assembly floor, which he did yesterday.

Mr. Knight apologized and then appealed to lawmakers to put the incident behind them so that they could get on with the business of the day.

Wait one minute.

We'd like to get on with the business of the day, but everytime you look up somebody else is making another racist remark.

Jimmy the Greek, Al Campanis, Marge Schott...I could go on and on.

If you ask me, the Latino caucus let this guy off too easy. I mean some of these guys still don't get it.

Time out for sweeping stuff under the rug...it's time to clean house.

Just a thought. I'm Tavis Smiley.

And The Winner Is...?

(Part One)

May 5, 1993

Yesterday, attorney Stan Sanders endorsed conservative Republican Richard Riordan in the Los Angeles mayor's race.

Sanders, you'll recall, was the top-finishing Black candidate in the April primary.

Sanders only received 4% of the vote citywide, but garnered some 17% of the votes cast in the three city council districts with the most African American voters.

Explaining his endorsement, Sanders said he was supporting Riordan in part because he felt Riordan would win the June election.

Ironically, many of us voted for Stan Sanders in the primary even though we knew he could not win.

We did so because we supported his platform and wanted the brother to have a strong showing.

When you consider that Riordan received an anemic 10% of Sanders' core constituency — the Black vote — the Sanders-Riordan alliance doesn't make much sense.

A very shrewd political move on Sanders' part, but unfortunately doesn't speak well of an allegiance to his supporters.

More on this tomorrow.

Just a thought. I'm Tavis Smiley.

And The Winner Is...?

(Part Two)

May 6, 1993

Yesterday, I talked about the endorsement of conservative Republican Richard Riordan by attorney Stan Sanders in the Los Angeles mayor's race.

In the April primary, Sanders garnered 17% of the votes cast in the three city council districts with the most African American voters, and was the top-finishing Black candidate in the primary.

Clearly, while the endorsement of Riordan may have benefitted Sanders personally, it did nothing for his supporters politically.

Too often, Black elected officials and in this case would-be-office-holders, solicit our support during the primary campaign and then barter away that support during the general election.

To be sure, Riordan paid a price for Sanders' endorsement.

I won't speculate on what the asking price was, but how could Sanders endorse a candidate for mayor who received 10% of the votes among his core constituency?

At the very least, Sanders should have taken a page out of the Mark Ridley-Thomas playbook and extracted a detailed list of commitments from Riordan, like Ridley-Thomas did when he endorsed Mike Woo.

As it stands, I almost feel like my vote for Stan Sanders in the primary was wasted.

Just a thought. I'm Tavis Smiley.

Policing the Police
(Part One)

June 1, 1993

Last week, Miami police officer William Lozano was acquitted on manslaughter charges stemming from the shooting deaths of two Black men in 1989.

The controversial shooting was followed by three days of rioting in Miami four years ago.

In recent days, this retrial of Lozano had been likened to the second trial of the four LAPD officers then accused of beating Rodney King.

Prior to the verdict, police were on full alert in riot gear and six National Guard units were called up.

While Miami remained calm, it must be said that the absence of another riot is not necessarily the presence of justice...not to mention economic or political empowerment.

We must reject the notion that because there is calm in the city, all is well. Like Los Angeles, Miami is a sick city in need of major surgery.

At best, the increased police presence only acts as a painkiller. Openly express your "pain" in the wrong way, and you just might get "killed."

More on this tomorrow.

Just a thought. I'm Tavis Smiley.

Policing the Police

(Part Two)

June 2, 1993

Yesterday, I told you that authorities in Miami, Florida, braced themselves last Friday night for rioting in the streets.

Late last week, a Miami police officer was acquitted in a retrial for the shooting deaths of two Black men four years ago.

The shooting precipitated three days of rioting in 1989. Taking a page out of the Los Angeles playbook, Miami police were in riot gear on full alert Friday night and six National Guard units were also called up.

Now, for all the things Black folks are, we are not suicidal.

Anyone facing a militia of police and National Guard troops could be convinced to show a little restraint.

All the focus on the riot aversion deflects conversation about what really causes these uprisings in the first place. Feelings of hopelessness, neglect, and systematic disenfranchisement by a growing number of Americans.

We ignore this reality at our own peril.

Just a thought. I'm Tavis Smiley.

Wrong Shade of Brown

June 11, 1993

Kathleen Brown wants to be the next governor of California. As state treasurer, Ms. Brown has been quite good on women's issues...but why are there no Mexican-Americans, no African Americans and only one Asian-American on the Treasurer's personal staff?

Why have only three state financings been senior managed by firms owned and operated by people of color during Ms. Brown's tenure as state treasurer?

Why have financial institutions owned by people of color earned such a minuscule percentage of all investment transaction fees done by the treasurer's office?

And why in only two state financings has the treasurer's office under Kathleen Brown retained law firms owned by people of color as sole bond counsel?

California's growing ethnic constituency is entitled to its share of the economic pie. We've been nibbling at crumbs from the Republican table...but what are the Democrats offering now — crust?

Like you no doubt, I'm tired of voting for the lesser of two evils.

For once...just once...I'd like to choose a candidate without having to flip a coin.

Just a thought. I'm Tavis Smiley.

Resign or Withdraw

May 18, 1993

Recently, President Clinton nominated a man named Webb Hubbell for the No. 3 job at the Justice Department.

Hubbell, a longtime friend of the Clinton's, has been a member of the Country Club of Little Rock since 1985.

Until last year, the private club did not admit African Americans. In December, the Arkansas club admitted its first Black member, but only after then candidate-Clinton played golf there and caused a national uproar about all-White clubs.

Until now, Mr. Hubbell has refused to resign his club membership or withdraw his nomination.

Hubbell has denied any knowledge of discriminatory policies by the club, yet claims that once a member he worked hard to integrate the country club.

Figure that one out.

Mr. Hubbell's hearings begin today in Washington, and some senators have already suggested that Mr. Hubbell resign if he wants the job.

So...we force Mr. Hubbell to resign his membership from a club that discriminates against people of color, so that we can make him the No. 3 man in the Justice Department?

I'm through with it.

Just a thought. I'm Tavis Smiley.

The Peoples' Choice
(Part One)

June 24, 1993

One week from today, Tom Bradley will surrender his title as mayor after twenty years of service.

History, of course, will be the final arbiter of the Bradley Administration's effectiveness. For his part, Tom Bradley has said that next week he will leave City Hall for the last time as mayor, secure in the knowledge that although he did not accomplish all that he set out to do, he tried his very best.

Well, sometimes Mayor Bradley's best surpassed all our hopes and expectations. Who could forget the 1984 Summer Olympic Games?

Still other times, the mayor's best just wasn't good enough. Consider the flap regarding Mayor Bradley's personal finances and accusations of influence peddling.

Not to worry...history has a way of reconciling fact with fiction.

Many have suggested that the so-called "Bradley coalition" is also a thing of the past. As evidence, they point to the racial divide in the recent mayoral race to succeed Tom Bradley.

I beg to differ.

Without question, the coalition which first elected Tom Bradley in 1973 is more viable today than it was twenty years ago. Whether Los Angeles can ever produce another person worthy of the support of these divergent groups remains to be seen.

More on this tomorrow.

Just a thought. I'm Tavis Smiley.

The Peoples' Choice
(Part Two)

June 25, 1993

Next week Tom Bradley will leave City Hall for the last time as mayor.

Tom Bradley has quietly brought diverse people together his entire life. When you think about it, Bradley is in part responsible for the unlikely alliance between Mayor-elect Richard Riordan and African American attorney Stan Sanders.

Sanders, the most visible and influential person of color on the Riordan transition team, became closely acquainted with Mr. Riordan as a member of the city's Recreation and Parks Commission where the two men served as Bradley appointees.

Tom Bradley has left far more than the downtown skyline or the mass transit system.

Tom Bradley opened the channels of communication for the people who comprise the most culturally and ethnically diverse city in the world to talk to one another.

I speak with some authority.

As a college student, I interned for Mayor Bradley. Later I served as his administrative aide. Today I have the good fortune of being able to share my thoughts with you.

Thanks Mr. B.

Just a thought. I'm Tavis Smiley.

What's Next...Forced Abortions?
(Part One)

February 18, 1993

Today in America, 619 female teenagers became sexually active...1,169 children were born out of wedlock...and 269 kids between the ages of 15 and 19 had abortions.

Some have suggested that the answer to these social ills is the use of a contraceptive called Norplant.

This device consists of six, match-stick size capsules that are surgically implanted in a woman's arm.

These capsules release a low-level dose of a synthetic hormone used in some birth control pills.

Studies show that Norplant is very effective in preventing pregnancy for a period of five years.

It seems to me that as part of the growing debate about Norplant we need to first discuss the need for values education which stresses abstinence.

A comprehensive values education program would change many of the statistics I cited earlier, thereby reducing the need for Norplant.

Tomorrow...why some government officials want to do more than make Norplant available — they want to mandate it for certain women.

Just a thought. I'm Tavis Smiley.

What's Next...Forced Abortions?
(Part Two)

February 19, 1993

Thirteen states have now proposed legislation that would use Norplant, an implantable contraceptive, as a tool of social policy.

One politician in Mississippi proposed that Norplant be required for any woman with at least four children who seeks state assistance.

Two weeks ago, Maryland governor Donald Schaefer made headlines when he suggested that welfare mothers either get Norplanted...or get off the dole.

In Tennessee, officials wanted to pay women on welfare $500 to get Norplant and $50 a year for each year they kept it.

As far as I'm concerned, this kind of misguided social policy smacks of state-sponsored genocide upon the poor, because it mandates the reproductive behavior of those who depend upon the state for support.

This notion of forced contraception by the state is extremely troubling.

When government starts controlling reproductive rights, the next step may very well be forced abortions.

Just a thought. I'm Tavis Smiley.

Six Months Later...

October 30, 1992

The six month anniversary of the country's worst urban civil disorder has brought on a flurry of recent news stories.

I read an interesting statistic the other day. In May, following Los Angeles' civil unrest, the number of stories on urban America broadcast over the three major television networks jumped to 37. Up from just 3 news stories in the month preceding.

The total slipped to 29 stories in June, 12 in July, and 7 in August.

As the media lost interest, so too did all the Washington politicians who talked about an urban aid package for Los Angeles.

Talk is about all they did. Immediately following the civil disorder, a $9 to 12 billion emergency aid package was discussed in the House.

What actually became law was a watered-down $1 billion measure that provided summer jobs, flood relief for Chicago and some small business loans.

And we thought burning down the city had gotten the attention of our local, state and federal elected officials.

As usual, when all was said and done, more was said than done.

Next Tuesday is about holding people accountable. I know I can't wait to get in the voting booth.

Just a thought. I'm Tavis Smiley.

Someday

April 2, 1993

This Sunday, April 4th, marks the 25th anniversary of the assassination of Dr. Martin Luther King, Jr.

But 25 years after King's death, the struggle for civil and human rights continues in this country.

I guess that's why I have a problem holding hands and singing, "We Shall Overcome" someday.

I don't know when "someday" is.

I'm familiar with Sunday, Tuesday or Friday. But when is someday?

Well, someday soon President Clinton will announce his nominee to replace retiring Supreme Court Justice Byron White.

Clinton has said he will appoint the most qualified person with the character to serve on the high court.

Quite frankly, it represents a lack of character to have a Supreme Court with no gender or ideological balance and almost no color.

President Clinton has a unique opportunity to select an individual who will provide diversity and make the court look more like America — today.

Just a thought. I'm Tavis Smiley.